CREATING WITH

SHEET PLASTIC

By Gregg LeFevre
Photographs by the Author

**LITTLE
CRAFT BOOK
SERIES**

 STERLING PUBLISHING CO., INC. NEW YORK

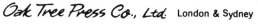 Oak Tree Press Co., Ltd. London & Sydney

Little Craft Book Series

ACKNOWLEDGMENT

Illus. 45 on page 25 has been reproduced through the courtesy of the Rohm and Haas Company.

Copyright © 1974 by Sterling Publishing Co., Inc.
419 Park Avenue South, New York, N.Y. 10016
Distributed in Canada by Saunders of Toronto, Ltd., Don Mills, Ontario
British edition published by Oak Tree Press Co., Ltd., Nassau, Bahamas
Distributed in Australia and New Zealand by Oak Tree Press Co., Ltd.,
P.O. Box J34, Brickfield Hill, Sydney 2000, N.S.W.
Distributed in the United Kingdom and elsewhere in the British Commonwealth
by Ward Lock Ltd., 116 Baker Street, London W 1
Manufactured in the United States of America   *All rights reserved*
Library of Congress Catalog Card No.: 74–82326
Sterling ISBN 0-8069-5314-4 Trade   Oak Tree 7061-2033-7
5315-2 Library

Contents

Before You Begin

Sheet plastic is an amazingly versatile, light-weight, and durable acrylic material. It can be easily used to make any number of useful and attractive items for your home, classroom, or office. Each of the three largest manufacturers of sheet plastic markets its product under a trade name, and you should know some names when shopping for the material.

For example, "Plexiglas" is made by the Rohm and Haas Co. ("Oroglas" in England and Australia) and "Acrylite" is made by the American Cyanamid Co.

Generally, sheet plastic is available at hardware dealers' and at glass and building supply houses, as well as from craft supply shops. You might also check to see if there is a plastics distributor in your vicinity. These distributors usually carry sheet-plastic scraps too, and *you can do many of the projects in this book with scrap material.* This is considerably less expensive than the new sheets. Companies which make sheet-plastic furniture and accessories might also have scrap, and many times they will let you have some free.

Acrylic is available in a wide variety of forms, textures, colors, and patterns. Sheet plastic comes in standard thicknesses of $\frac{1}{10}''$, $\frac{1}{8}''$, $\frac{1}{4}''$, and $\frac{1}{2}''$ (2.5 mm., 3 mm., 6 mm., and 12.5 mm.). Many dealers sell it by the square foot in sizes up to $48'' \times 72''$ (142 × 218 cm.). Probably the easiest to work with for most of the projects in this book are the $\frac{1}{8}''$ (3 mm.) and $\frac{1}{4}''$ (6 mm.) thicknesses.

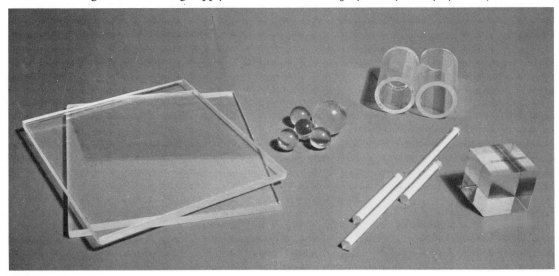

Illus. 1. Here are some of the forms in which acrylic is manufactured. From left to right are: sheets, balls, tubes, rods, and a block of cast acrylic.

These are neither too thin nor too thick for you to handle. Sheet plastic can be transparent, translucent, or opaque, and a number of different colors are available. Also, it is manufactured with several different surface patterns that reflect or bend light for decorative effects. Although clear sheet plastic was used for all of the projects pictured in this book, keep in mind that you can use any kind you wish with the same results.

Besides acrylic in sheet form, tubing, rods, blocks, balls, beads, and pellets are also available—all of which you can use in conjunction with sheet if you wish. You can also buy damaged or scrap pieces of tubing at low cost and you can cut the good sections out of these for use in some of your projects. All of the various forms have exactly the same properties as sheets.

This book offers you simple directions for all the procedures you will need to know in order to make a variety of things with sheet plastic, along with a great number of suggestions for specific projects you might want to try to make or use as a basis for a project of your own.

The first project is a simple letter opener, but in making it, you will learn how to cut sheet plastic—the first step in nearly every project. You will find out about drilling and finishing by making a hanging plant holder, about cementing as you assemble a bud vase or aquarium, and about fastening pieces of sheet together with nuts, bolts and screws to make an attractive picture frame.

Next, you learn how to create simple items which require you to *bend* the sheet. Such bends can be made by heating the plastic over an ordinary light bulb. More complicated bending, necessary for many projects, requires a strip heater, and you

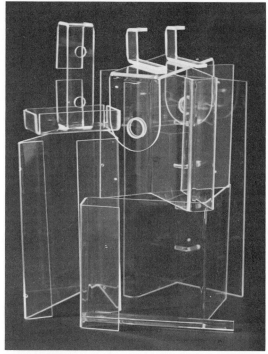

Illus. 2. This may look like a modern sculpture, but if you look closely you will see many of the projects you will be making in this book—book-ends, pencil tray, and so on.

will learn here how you can make your own heater.

Finally, you will find a number of more advanced projects which call for all of the procedures you will have learned—cutting, drilling, attaching, and bending. By the time you have completed just a few of these projects, you should be able to make your own original creations with sheet plastic!

5

Illus. 3. Lay out your designs right on the protective masking paper that covers sheet plastic.

Illus. 4. Do not remove the masking paper from the acrylic sheet until after you have cut, drilled, and finished any rough edges.

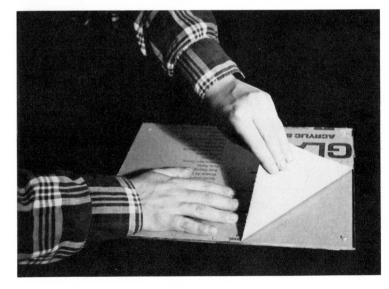

Handling Sheet Plastic

You must be careful about how you handle sheet plastic after you acquire it. You should store it in a clean dry place where the temperature does not go above normal room temperature. Store it either in a completely vertical or a completely flat, horizontal position, because if it is left leaning against something at an angle, or hanging over an edge, it has a tendency to bend or warp.

As it comes from a dealer, sheet plastic is covered with a protective paper masking on both sides. Usually, the name of the manufacturer and some information about the product is printed on the wrapping. Even though you are anxious to look at the plastic underneath, you should leave the wrapping in place. The masking protects the plastic from being nicked and scratched *while* you are working with it.

If you have purchased sheet or scrap without this masking, then it is a good idea to wrap it in newspaper, tissue paper, or cloth until you are ready to use it.

The rule-of-thumb is to treat a sheet of plastic as carefully as you would a sheet of glass, even though it is far more durable. If you do, you will ensure a clear, unblemished surface on your finished products.

Laying Out Your Design

Once you have decided upon a project, and know what size pieces you will need, you must mark off the sections to be cut. Do this with a pencil or soft-tip ink marker and a ruler, marking off the lines to be cut right on the masking paper.

Or, if the masking paper has been removed, use a china-marking pencil, or a soft-tip pen right on the sheet-plastic surface. Any of these marks remaining on the finished object can be cleaned off easily.

Cleaning Sheet Plastic

The best way to clean sheet plastic is to use warm, soapy water, and either your bare hands or a soft rag or sponge. After cleaning, wipe the sheet dry with a lint-free cloth or tissue.

Do not use window cleaners, abrasive soaps, paint thinners, or carbon tetrachloride on acrylic! If soapy water will not remove grease or other dirt, try wiping it off with kerosene or acetone. Then wash over it again with soapy water.

Safety Rules

1. Be careful handling the sharp edges of freshly cut sheet and also of the tools you are using. Wearing gloves is a good idea.

2. When using solvent cement, work in a well-ventilated area. Do *not* work near a flame or someone smoking, and avoid getting the cement on your hands or face.

3. When working with a strip heater, *always* unplug it immediately after use so that you do not forget it. Also, it is a good idea to have a sign on the heater which says "Danger—Hot."

4. Do not overheat sheet plastic. At high temperatures it is combustible, although it burns slowly.

5. Be careful when working with hand or power tools. Always be sure that your sheet plastic is firmly held down.

Illus. 5. Use a sharp-pointed metal tool to score the sheet plastic along the line you intend to "cut."

Cutting Sheet Plastic

A letter opener such as the one in Illus. 12 is one of the simplest objects you can make with sheet plastic. The first step is to cut a strip of plastic about $8'' \times \frac{3}{4}''$ (200 $\times$ 18 mm.).

There are several ways to cut sheet plastic. Sheet up to $\frac{1}{4}''$ (6 mm.) thick can be snapped along a scribed line in much the same fashion as glass is "cut." Run a scriber or other sharp-pointed metal instrument along a straightedge or ruler several times in order to score a deep scratch into the surface of the plastic.

Then break the scored sheet in one of two ways. Either place the scored line face-up, directly over the edge of a table or work-bench and press down on the overhanging section, or place it with the scored line face-up over a $\frac{3}{4}''$ (18 mm.) dowel, and apply pressure downwards on either side of the scored line.

Illus. 6. One way to break the scribed sheet is to place the scored line directly over a table edge and press down.

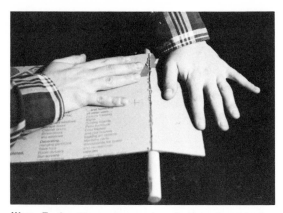

Illus. 7. Another way to break the sheet is by simply rolling it over a ¾" (18 mm.) dowel, at the same time pressing down on both sides of the scored line.

You can also use handsaws or power saws to cut sheet plastic. In general, a sharp, fine-toothed saw blade designed for cutting metals such as brass, copper, or aluminum works best. Whether you use a handsaw (such as a hack-saw, a coping saw, or a jewelry saw) or a power saw (such as a sabre saw, band saw, jigsaw, or circular saw), the saw-blade teeth should be uniform in height, have the same shape, and have the same "rake" (Illus. 9).

Whichever type of saw you use, there are several rules to follow. First of all, do not remove the masking paper before you cut. It will protect the surface of your sheet plastic from scratches while you saw.

Second, if you are not sure whether your saw

Illus. 9. Whatever kind of saw you use, be sure the teeth are uniform.

Illus. 8. You can cut sheet plastic with handsaws or power saw if you have one available. Here, a hack-saw is being used to cut along the scribed line.

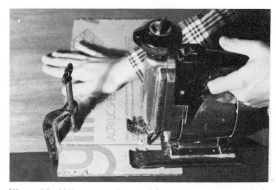

Illus. 10. When cutting with a power saw, such as this sabre saw, use a vice to hold the sheet down firmly.

Illus. 11. A V-board support is ideal for cutting out special designs, and you can easily make one yourself.

blade is suited to the job, test it out by cutting some scrap or damaged pieces first.

Third, be sure that your sheet is well supported on a flat surface and is securely held down with some sort of clamp before you begin cutting. This will prevent chattering and chipping.

Finally, use a piece of cardboard or several thicknesses of paper to protect the plastic where the clamps are to be applied.

If you use power tools in cutting, there are a few more important rules to keep in mind. Never force-feed the sheet—heat will build up and the plastic round the cut will melt, causing the saw blade to gum up and stick. Also, stop now and then during the cutting to allow the blade to cool. Finally, if you are using a circular saw, set the blade height just a hair wider than the thickness of the sheet in order to get the cleanest cut.

For cutting out curves or intricate patterns, a V-board support to go under the sheet is a helpful device. You can make one easily from $\frac{3}{4}''$ (18 mm.) plywood (Illus. 11). This handy board will allow you to cut freely while it supports the sheet plastic.

Letter Opener

When you have cut out the basic piece for the letter opener, a strip of plastic 8″ × $\frac{3}{4}''$ (200 × 18 mm.), you must next saw off the corners to form a point, as shown in Illus. 12. Cut diagonally from the midpoint of one end of the strip to points about 2″ (50 mm.) back along each side. Remove the masking paper, and wrap new masking tape around 3″ (75 mm.) of the strip at the end away from the point. The tape will protect the handle while you file down the pointed part until this becomes a thin, pointed, bladelike section. Use the same kind of flat file you would use on metal for coarse filing, then sandpaper wrapped around a flat block of wood for the final smoothing.

Then pull off the tape, lightly sand only the edges of the handle, and your opener is ready to use.

Illus. 12. To make this handsome letter opener, you need only cut, file, and sand a strip of sheet plastic.

Drilling Sheet Plastic

The next technique to learn is how to make holes in plastic sheet. You can use either a hand drill or a power drill. With a hand drill, or a brace and a bit, use a regular twist bit (the kind used to drill metal) as shown in Illus. 13. The sheet you are drilling should be firmly supported, the protective wrapping paper should not be removed, and the place to be drilled should be marked with a china-marking pencil or a scriber. Never use a center punch—it will only crack the sheet plastic.

Illus. 13. If you drill with a hand drill, be sure to use a regular twist bit.

Illus. 14. Whether you use a hand drill or a power drill, be sure the sheet plastic is firmly held and supported.

Illus. 15. This hanging plant and its pot are supported by a square of sheet plastic. All you need to do is cut and drill to make one like it.

Plant Hanger

To make a plant hanger, start with a 3″ (75 mm.) square of sheet plastic and drill a hole near each of the four corners of the square (Illus. 16).

Now, decide how far down you want your plant to hang, and cut two pieces of string, cord,

wire, or chain, $2\frac{1}{2}$ times that length. Run one piece down through a corner hole and up through the corner hole diagonally opposite it. Do the same with the second piece, using the other two holes.

Next, tie all four ends together with a secure knot. You can now insert the pot by placing the plastic square under the middle of its bottom, and running up the four tying strings equally spaced along the side of the pot.

Illus. 16. Here is the simple hanger, with its four holes drilled in the corners and a piece of wire threaded through them in a criss-cross fashion.

Illus. 17. See these charming hanging candle holders in color on the front cover.

Hanging Candle Holders

You can make the hanging candle holders in Illus. 17 in much the same fashion as the preceding plant hanger, except for two differences. First, do not run the hanging wires down through the hole in one corner and then up through the corner hole diagonally opposite it. Instead, run them down through a corner hole and up through the one on the next corner.

Second, you need to cut a hole in the middle of the square for the candle glass. Cut this hole after you have definitely decided on what type of glass and candle you will want. Your candle glass must be wider at the top than at the bottom so that it will not fall through the hole!

After you have marked off the area to be cut out, drill a hole inside the outline and pass the blade of a coping saw or a hacksaw through it.

If you find cutting a circular hole too difficult, you can cut a square hole for the candle glass, but measure and cut it very accurately or else the glass may not rest evenly.

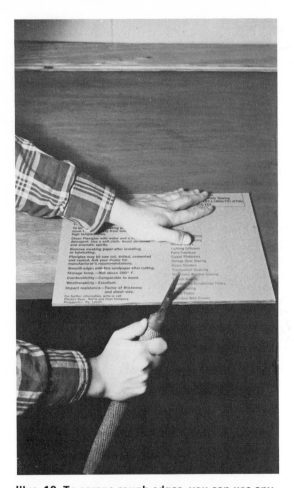

Illus. 18. To scrape rough edges, you can use any tool that has a square sharp edge, such as the end of this file. Be sure never to remove the masking tape from the sheet plastic until you have completed all such procedures, so that you will not mar the surface.

Finishing Sheet Plastic

There are several steps in the finishing procedure, and the one you choose will depend upon the type of finish you want.

To finish rough edges, scrape them with any metal tool that has a square sharp edge. A knife blade or the tang of a file will work well. Hold the metal scraper at a 45° angle to the surface of the edge being scraped (Illus. 18).

After scraping, sand the edge, using sandpaper wrapped round a block of wood (Illus. 19). Be sure the block is flat and hold it at a 90° angle to the sheet so as to keep the edge square. If you want a transparent finish on your edges, start with medium-grained paper and work up to very fine-grained paper, such as #600.

If you wish a perfectly clear finish, use a polishing compound after sanding. Jewelers' paste, copper cleaner, or pumice and water work well as polishers. Apply them with a soft rag and a good deal of hand rubbing (Illus. 20), or with a buffing wheel on a power drill.

Use the same procedures for eliminating marks or scratches on the surface of sheet plastic as well. If such abrasions are deep, it may be wise to sand and buff the whole surface of the sheet, rather than have an indentation where you rubbed out the abrasion.

Automotive wax (the non-cleansing kind) can also be applied to sheet plastic to help hide scratches. A coat of such wax will help to protect the plastic from future scratches and nicks as well.

Illus. 19. After the edges have been scraped smooth, use sandpaper wrapped round a block of wood to attain a fine finish.

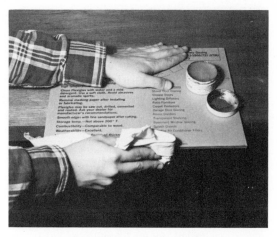

Illus. 20. Polish edges to get a transparent finish. You can do this by hand with a soft rag or with a buffing wheel on a power tool.

Cementing Sheet Plastic

It is easy to glue two pieces of sheet plastic together to form a strong, transparent bond. However, some care and practice is necessary to achieve good results. Illus. 21 to 24 show four types of cemented joints. As you can see, the *method* you choose will depend upon the objects you are glueing; however, in all cases, you need a special cement since regular household cement does not bond well. The special cement for glueing sheet plastic is actually a solvent cement which dissolves both of the surfaces being joined, and when it evaporates, the two surfaces become a single unit.

No matter what type of cementing method you

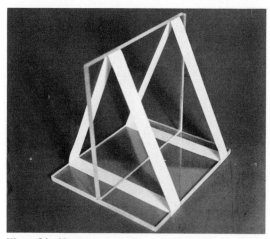

Illus. 21. If you are going to cement a T-joint, use this arrangement to hold the sheets in place.

15

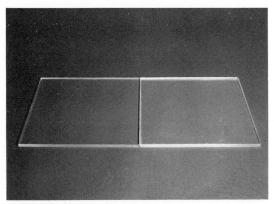

Illus. 22. This is a simple butt joint. You might place two heavy blocks at each end, however, when you are cementing.

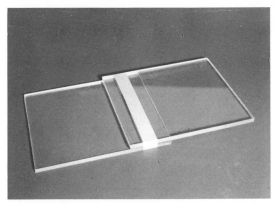

Illus. 23. When cementing an overlapping joint, tape the two pieces tightly together in this fashion.

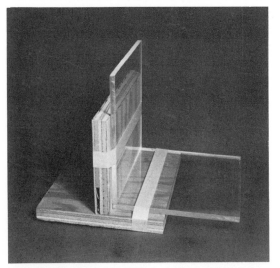

Illus. 24. With certain joints, such as this L-joint, you will need to use a more elaborate arrangement of blocks and tape to hold the sheets together while cementing.

use, there are certain procedures to follow. First of all, set up your support braces, clamps, or whatever, ahead of time and check that they hold the pieces you are glueing firmly in the positions that you want. Sometimes a simple arrangement with masking tape or a couple of blocks of wood will serve. At other times, more elaborate arrangements of blocks and clamps, or even two pieces of wood nailed together to form a 90° angle, are necessary.

Second, do not heavily sand and polish the surfaces to be glued. This might result in rounded edges, which could not form a tight joint.

Third, keep these safety measures in mind when cementing: 1. Work in a well-ventilated space and avoid breathing the cement fumes. 2. Do not work near a flame or someone smoking because the solvent cement is flammable. 3. Avoid getting the cement on your skin. If you do, wash with soap and water as soon as possible.

Capillary Cementing

This is the best method for cementing edges which fit together perfectly. Sand the edges *very lightly*. Then position them tightly together, using whichever arrangement is necessary to give them firm support. Next, using either an eye-dropper, a fine brush, a syringe, or a squeeze bottle fitted with a fine nozzle, carefully apply the solvent cement along the seam between the two tightly fitting pieces.

A phenomenon called "capillary action" will draw in the cement. After 30 seconds, the cement should be working, and you can apply pressure to the joint to force out any air bubbles. Now, position a weight of some sort on the joint so as to maintain this pressure, and leave the joint alone for 24 hours to dry completely.

Illus. 26. Soak-cementing is suitable for joining edges that do not have to fit together perfectly.

Illus. 25. Capillary cementing is the best way to cement together edges which must fit exactly.

Soak-Cementing

If the edges you intend to join do not fit together perfectly, the soak method works better than capillary cementing. However, if there are uneven gaps, viscous (thickened) cement or all-acrylic cement are better still. (See page 18.)

To soak-cement, first apply a smooth, flat layer of masking tape almost up to the edge to be joined. Next, soak the edge in a shallow container of the solvent. Rest the edge being soaked on several pins, so that it does not stick to the bottom of the container (Illus. 26).

Sometime between 30 seconds and several minutes, the edge will begin to soften and swell. Once this happens, remove it from the solvent

Illus. 27. You can make this lovely bud vase simply by cementing a piece of plastic tubing to a small square of sheet plastic.

and quickly bring it into contact with the other edge to be joined. Then place both pieces in the support set-up you have devised. The solvent on the soaked piece will dissolve the edge of the dry piece somewhat, forming the bond. As with capillary cementing, allow the pieces to sit for

30 seconds or so before you apply pressure to force out any air bubbles. Allow 24 hours for it to dry completely.

Thickened Cement

You can make your own thickened cement, suitable for joining pieces which do not have evenly fitting joints. Simply dissolve small clean chips of sheet plastic in solvent cement and let the solution thicken overnight. Then brush the cement on the edges and proceed as in soak-cementing.

All-Acrylic Cement and Epoxy Cement

A number of other cements are available which you can use to join pieces of sheet plastic. All-acrylic and clear epoxy are two such cements. They are also well suited for joining pieces of sheet that do not have close-fitting joints. With either of these cements, follow the label instructions carefully. Avoid cements which are not specifically recommended for use with acrylic sheet.

Bud Vase

There are any number of objects you can make by combining tubing and sheet. The bud vase in Illus. 27 is probably the easiest.

Cut a 5″ (125 mm.) section of tubing with a diameter anywhere from ½″ to 1″ (12.5 to 25 mm.). Next, smooth both ends and make certain that the edges of one end lie in a perfectly flat plane. Then cut a 3″ (75 mm.) square of sheet plastic. Place the tubing, with its smoothest end down, in the exact middle of the square sheet you cut, and glue it. As with all glueing, place a weight of some sort on top and allow 24 hours for it to dry thoroughly.

Aquarium

You make the aquarium shown in Illus. 28 in exactly the same way as the bud vase in Illus. 27. The only difference is the size. Use a 6″ (150 mm.) diameter tube, 18″ (450 mm.) long, and make the bottom square sheet 8″ × 8″ (200 × 200 mm.). (Larger-diameter tubing is even better if you can find it, but you will also have to make a larger bottom square to accommodate it, if you do.)

Illus. 28. This unique aquarium is similar to the bud vase in Illus. 27, but larger.

Fastening Sheet Plastic

with

Nuts, Bolts, and Screws

Two plastic sheets can be bolted together to form attractive, see-through picture or photo frames. Do this simply by drilling a hole slightly larger than the shaft of the bolt you are going to use. Insert the bolt and thread the nut on. Be careful not to overtighten the nut, for the plastic will crack if you do.

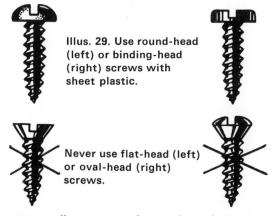

Illus. 29. Use round-head (left) or binding-head (right) screws with sheet plastic.

Never use flat-head (left) or oval-head (right) screws.

You will want to attach some sheet-plastic items to a wall or door with screws. However, only round-head- or binding-head- (sheet metal) screws are well suited for use with sheet plastic. Flat-head or oval-head screws with tapered heads should *not* be used because they will crack the area round any hole they are turned into.

19

Illus. 30. A sheet-plastic frame provides an ideal setting for paintings, prints, or other objects you wish to display.

Hanging Frames, Pictures, or Designs

If you want to hang a sheet-plastic frame, picture, or design you have made, there are a number of ways to do it.

The simplest way is to drill a hole in the top middle of your sheet (Illus. 31) and hang it on a nail or hook.

Another way is to drill two holes on the top of your sheet and run a loop of wire between them (Illus. 32).

You can also drill two holes, thread two short screws directly into the plastic, and run a wire between them (Illus. 33). Make sure that the holes you drill are larger than the solid shafts of the screws you are using but slightly smaller than the outside width of the threads. Use soap or wax on the holes before turning in the screws. Unlike wood, acrylic does not give when a screw is turned into it—it cracks instead.

If you want to screw two pieces of sheet plastic together, use machine screws with coarse threads.

Finally, you can make a hanging bar of $\frac{1}{8}''$

Illus. 31. One method of hanging a frame is by drilling a hole in the exact middle of the top and then placing it over a nail in the wall.

Illus. 32. An alternative is to drill two holes and loop a wire through them.

thick (3 mm.) sheet (Illus. 34). Cut and glue two small sheet-plastic squares to the back of your project. Then, glue on a bar running between them as shown.

Illus. 34. An attractive hanging arrangement is this small sheet-plastic bar glued onto the sheet-plastic frame.

Scrap Wall Design

You can make many types of wall decorations, such as the one in Illus. 35, by cementing scraps of sheet plastic onto a larger piece of sheet. You might also want to include sections of tubing or rod, or some other scrap materials, such as wood or fabric. In addition, colored sheet plastic or pieces of colored glass can be cemented on sections of sheet to give a stained-glass-window effect.

Illus. 35.

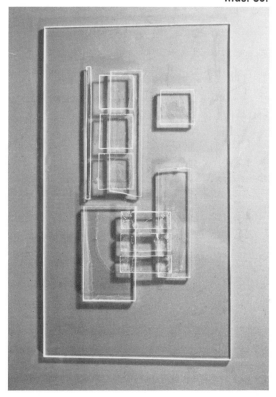

Picture Frames

You may wish to frame something you have painted or drawn, or a photo or print. To make the type of frame shown in Illus. 37, simply bolt together two sheets of plastic with whatever you wish to display in between. (See page 19 for bolting and hanging instructions.)

It is also possible to make a painting right on the surface of the sheet plastic. Use acrylic paint and

Illus. 36. Use machine screws with coarse threads when joining two pieces of sheet plastic together to make a collage such as this (see front cover).

Collage

Various kinds of collages can be mounted between two pieces of sheet plastic. You can create collages using natural materials, such as leaves, pressed flowers, or seashells. Or, make collages of colored cloth scraps, package and jar labels, or construction-paper cutouts.

The collage shown in Illus. 36 was made from magazine cutouts of clocks and watches.

Illus. 37. You can frame pictures between two sheets of plastic, or you can paint directly on a sheet, forming a frame by placing masking tape round the edges, then removing it after the paint has dried.

place masking tape round the four sides to make neat, clean borders. Remove the tape when the paint is dry.

You can make standing photo frames in two different styles. To make the two types of frames shown in Illus. 38, strip-heat an appropriate-sized piece of $\frac{1}{8}''$ (3 mm.) thick sheet and fold it into whichever style frame you choose (see below for instructions on heatforming).

Heatforming

The most unusual characteristic of sheet plastic is that when it is heated, it becomes pliable and can be bent into almost any shape, which it will retain upon cooling. This is called "heatforming." Generally, strip heaters are used to heat acrylic sheet for bending, but for heating strips of thin sheet, or thin acrylic rods, it is possible to use a regular incandescent light bulb.

Bulb Heating

Use a high-wattage bulb, which gives off more heat and so works better for this purpose.

Set up an arrangement so that the plastic material you are heating rests as close as possible to the bulb without touching it, such as in Illus. 39. Then, heat the plastic until it is soft enough to bend. (It is best to wear sun-glasses while working over the bulb to protect your eyes.) Once you have bent the material into the desired shape, either cool it in water, or clamp it down in position until it cools.

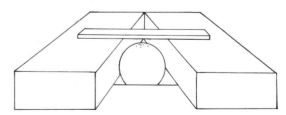

Illus. 39. This arrangement is best for bulb heating. Be sure the bulb does not touch the plastic material.

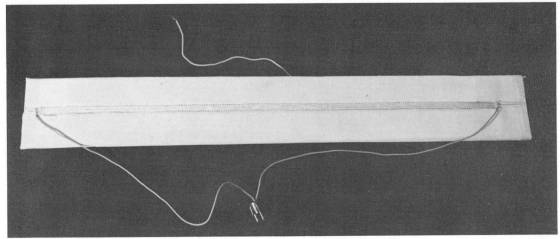

Illus. 40. A strip heater will heat a narrow section of your plastic sufficiently so that you can make a simple bend or fold.

Strip Heating

A strip heater warms up a narrow section of thin sheet plastic, allowing you to make a simple line bend. Regardless of the type of strip heater you may use, the principles of heatforming remain the same.

Illus. 41. When the sheet has become hot enough to bend, hold it like this.

Illus. 42. Then start your bending.

Cut your sheet plastic to the correct size for the project you are working on while it is still flat. When you are ready to bend the material, place it over the strip heater with the line for the bend just above the heating element. Do not let the acrylic material actually touch the heating element as that will create bubbles in the plastic, discolor it, or both. When the sheet along the line of the heating element becomes hot enough to be pliable, you can bend the sheet to whatever angle you desire. It is helpful to heat a narrow test strip of

24

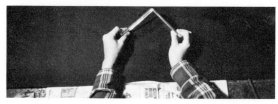

Illus. 43. Keep bending carefully until . . .

Illus. 44. . . . you have made a right angle.

sheet plastic alongside the good piece, so that you can test its pliability from time to time to learn when the piece for your project is ready to be bent.

As with glueing sheets together, it is wise to have your support set-up—blocks, clamps, or whatever—ready ahead of time so that once bent, the sheet can be immediately clamped to hold the position while it cools.

You can also cool a heatformed bend simply by dipping it into water. This saves time, but it is not as accurate as clamping the bend at exactly the correct angle. (Although water-cooling is supposed to weaken acrylic material, this did not seem to be a problem with any of the water-cooled pieces made for the projects in this book.)

To bend pieces of sheet plastic that are thicker than $\frac{1}{4}''$ (6 mm.), you must either flip the piece over so that it is heated on both sides, or use two strip heaters simultaneously—one above and one below.

Making a Strip Heater

You can purchase a strip heater, or you can make one yourself. Generally, dealers in sheet plastic also carry heating elements for a strip heater, or information on how to get them. Rohm and Haas, the company that makes Plexiglas, offers an inexpensive heating element and instructions on how to mount it (Illus. 45).

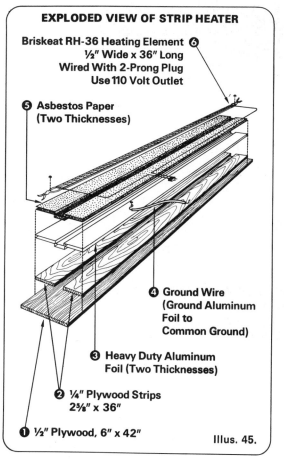

EXPLODED VIEW OF STRIP HEATER

Briskeat RH-36 Heating Element ❻
½″ Wide x 36″ Long
Wired With 2-Prong Plug
Use 110 Volt Outlet

❺ Asbestos Paper
(Two Thicknesses)

❹ Ground Wire
(Ground Aluminum
Foil to
Common Ground)

❸ Heavy Duty Aluminum
Foil (Two Thicknesses)

❷ ¼″ Plywood Strips
2⅝″ x 36″

❶ ½″ Plywood, 6″ x 42″

Illus. 45.

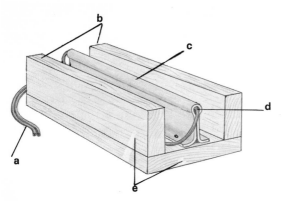

Illus. 46. A home-made strip heater. a. Electric wire. b. Wooden side supports slightly higher than heating element. c. Sheet-metal housing. d. Porcelain beads round Nichrome wire. e. Wood.

In addition, electrical supply houses, particularly those which deal in electrical-heating supplies, carry various types of strip-heating elements and electrical current regulators to go with them. These are generally more expensive than the type mentioned above.

Now, if you do not want to purchase a strip heater, it is possible for you to build one (Illus. 46). (Bear in mind, however, that commercial strip heaters are probably safer and do work better than one you can build yourself.)

As shown in Illus. 46, the heating element is made by running coiled Nichrome wire through porcelain beads. The beaded wire is then run through a piece of folded sheet metal and housed in an assembly like the one shown in the drawing. Current can then be run through the Nichrome wire.

26

Napkin Rings

Napkin rings can be made by heatforming sheet or rod over a light bulb or a strip heater. To make the ring in Illus. 47, use a strip of $\frac{1}{16}''$ (1.5 mm.) thick sheet cut to $\frac{1}{2}''$ (12.5 mm.) wide by 6" (150 mm.) long. Heat and then bend the strip 2" (50 mm.) in from first one end, then the other to form the triangular shape. Use these same proportions for any different-size holder you may want so that all sides of the triangle come out equal.

Make the ring in Illus. 48 by heating a 20" (500 mm.) long piece of $\frac{1}{8}''$ (3 mm.) rod. Heat the rod inch by inch, and as it softens, wind it round a $1\frac{1}{2}''$ (40 mm.) diameter cylinder. When finished, immerse it in water to cool it, and then cut off the ends which do not conform to the curve.

The ring in Illus. 49 was made by heating a 9" (225 mm.) long section of $\frac{1}{4}''$ (6 mm.) rod. Bend the rod into shape little by little, as it heats and softens.

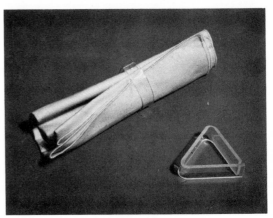

Illus. 47.

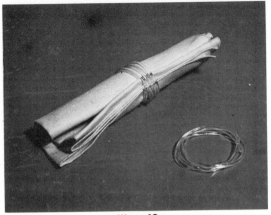

Illus. 48.

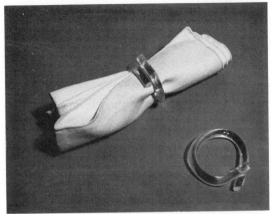

Illus. 49.

Jewelry

You can use thin sheet, $\frac{1}{16}''$ (1.5 mm.) thick combined with thin rod, $\frac{1}{16}''$ to $\frac{1}{8}''$ (1.5 to 3 mm.) thick, to make all sorts of simple jewelry by simply heatforming the plastic with either a light bulb or a strip heater.

Pendants

All of the sheet-plastic pendants shown in Illus. 50 to 52 were heatformed over a light bulb. Make the pendant in Illus. 50 by cutting out a triangular piece of sheet, $1\frac{1}{2}''$ (37.5 mm.) wide at the bottom and 5″ (125 mm.) long, narrowing to a point. Drill a hole at one of the corners away from the point. Then, heat and roll up the piece of sheet, starting with the square end and rolling towards the point. When the piece cools, run a chain through the hole.

Illus. 50. You can make this elegant pendant by simply heatforming a triangle of plastic over a light bulb.

Illus. 51.

Illus. 52.

You can make the pendants in Illus. 51 and 52 by heating long rectangular strips of sheet, 5″ × ½″ (125 × 12.5 mm.), with a hole drilled at one end. Form abstract designs by simply heating, then bending and twisting until you achieve an attractive shape.

Tie Clips

Tie clips like the three in Illus. 53 can also be heatformed with a light bulb. Cut out a strip of 1/16″ (1.5 mm.) thick sheet measuring 4″ × 5/8″ (100 × 15 mm.). Heat the strip near one end and bend it slightly to make the round back section of the clip. Then, heat it in the middle and fold the strip over on itself not quite all the way, so that you leave room for the tie to go in between.

Tie clips done in colored sheet plastic, or with small designs painted on them after heatforming are also very attractive. The small geometrical designs on the clips shown were painted on with acrylic paint.

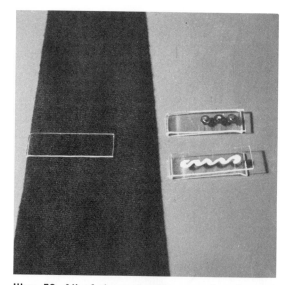

Illus. 53. All of these tie clips were heatformed over a light bulb. You might wish to use colored sheet plastic for your jewelry, although you can also paint designs on clear plastic, as was done here.

28

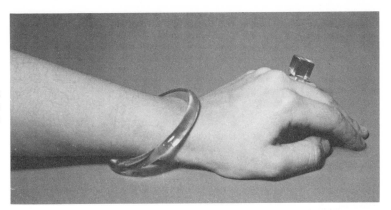

Illus. 54. This round bracelet was heatformed and then immediately wound round a cylinder to cool.

Bracelets and Rings

The round bracelet being worn in Illus. 54 can be made in a fashion similar to the spiral napkin ring in Illus. 49.

To make the bracelet, heat a $\frac{1}{4}''$ (6 mm.) rod or a narrow strip of $\frac{1}{8}''$ (3 mm.) thick sheet over a light bulb or strip heater, and then, inch by inch, as it softens, wind it round a wrist-sized cylinder. Use a cylinder of strong material such as a piece of pipe, or a tin can of the appropriate size. Afterwards, the wound plastic still has enough give so that the cylinder can be pulled out. A cylinder without a flange at the end is the easiest to remove. Once you have completed this, dip the plastic into water so that it will harden into this rounded shape.

You can make the rings in Illus. 54 and 55 by cutting off sections of tubing. Sand them smooth and glue on plastic jewels, pebbles, and so on.

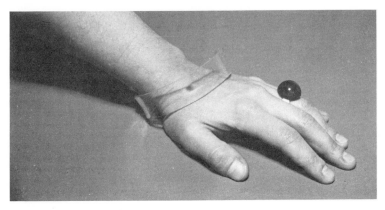

Illus. 55. Rings are easily made by cutting off pieces of tubing and glueing on artificial "gems" of various kinds.

29

Roundup of Practical Projects

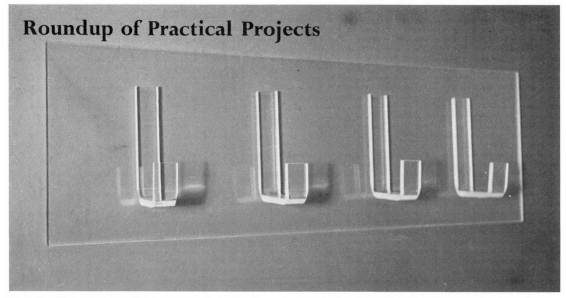

Illus. 56. Now that you have mastered the basic techniques of working with sheet plastic, you can try any number of interesting projects for your home, office, or classroom. A set of sheet-plastic clothes hooks would fit in any of these places!

You can put the techniques you have learned to use in making a variety of useful and decorative objects. You can alter the dimensions of these projects to suit your own needs or use these ideas as jumping-off points in creating your own plans.

Clothes Hooks

A set of handy plastic clothes hooks like the one in Illus. 56 is easy to make. They can be glued to a plastic backboard or individually mounted on a wall or closet door.

For each hook, cut out a rectangular strip from $\frac{1}{4}''$, $\frac{3}{8}''$, or $\frac{1}{2}''$ (6 mm., 10 mm., or 12.5 mm.) thick sheet plastic. Make each strip $7'' \times \frac{3}{4}''$ (175 × 20 mm.). You should mark and cut each strip separately, however, because the saw-blade removes a certain width of material with each cut and you need to allow for this. An easy way to do it is to make a cardboard pattern of just the right size, trace around it, and then cut out the first piece. Put the pattern down again with one edge flush with the edge of the sheet where you made the previous cut and repeat the procedure until you have cut out four identical strips (Illus. 57). Smooth and finish any rough edges.

Next, remove the protective masking paper from both sides of all four strips (Illus. 58). You will be making two bends in each strip and to ensure that all four pieces come out alike, you need to mark them carefully. Line up the four strips next to one another with their ends even, and draw a line across each, 1″ (25 mm.) from one end, another line 4″ (100 mm.) from the other end. Use a soft-tip ink marker or a china-marking pencil to do this.

Now, place all four strips on the strip heater, and heat them first along the line that you marked 1″ (25 mm.) from the end. Make sure that all the ends line up perfectly so that you will be heating and bending each strip in exactly the same place (Illus. 59).

When the strips have become hot enough so that they are pliable, bend a right angle in each along

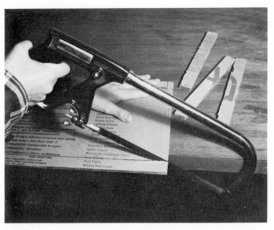

Illus. 57. Cutting the strips for hooks with a hack-saw.

Illus. 58. After cutting, remove the protective masking tape from the strips.

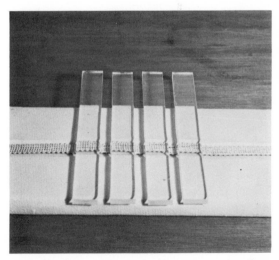

Illus. 59. Strip-heat each piece along the first line that you marked about 1″ (25 mm.) from each end.

Illus. 60. Start your right-angle bend along the first line you heated.

Illus. 61. Bend until it looks like this.

Illus. 62. After strip-heating each piece along the second line you marked 4″ (100 mm.) from each end, make another right angle like this.

the heated line (Illus. 61). Line them up so that the angles are the same. Then, secure each one in this position with clamps or blocks until it cools. If you have a good eye for angles, it is possible to simply bend the right angle and dip it in water to cool it. However, it may be difficult for you to do this accurately enough so that all four hooks are the same when finished.

Next, strip-heat all four strips in the same fashion as before along the line that you marked 4″ (100 mm.) from the end and bend another right angle along this line, so that each turns out looking like the hook in Illus. 62.

What you do next depends upon what type of clothes-hook arrangement you want. You can glue all four hooks onto a plastic backboard and mount that on your wall or closet door, or you can drill two holes in each hook and mount them individually.

Illus. 63. If you intend to glue your hooks to a backboard, use solvent cement.

If you decide to mount all four hooks on a backboard, begin by cutting out one which measures at least 5″ × 20″ (125 × 500 mm.). It can be made bigger if you wish. The one shown in Illus. 63 measures 8″ × 24″ (200 × 600 mm.). For mounting the backboard, drill a small hole in the same position in each of the two top corners of the backboard. Once all the edges have been finished, and the masking removed, decide where you want the hooks to go. They should be evenly spaced and all in a perfect line.

Next, glue down each hook using solvent cement. (Follow the procedures for cementing on page 15.) After allowing 24 hours for drying, your hook board is ready for mounting.

If you decide to mount your hooks individually, drill two holes, making the first hole 1″ (25 mm.), and the second hole 3″ (75 mm.) from the end, on the longest section, as shown in Illus. 64. Do this with all four hooks and they are ready for mounting. To mount the hooks, screw each one to a wall or door with round-head or binding-head screws (Illus. 65).

Illus. 64. If you mount your hooks individually, you must drill two holes in the long ends.

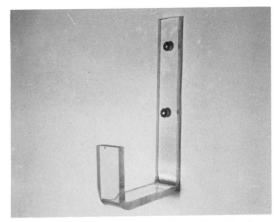

Illus. 65. Be sure to use round-head or binding-head screws to attach the hooks to a wall.

33

Illus. 66. The upright sections of these book-ends were painted with black acrylic paint.

Illus. 67. As any cook knows, recipe cards are subject to endless spattering and smudges from sticky fingers. A protective card holder made of sheet plastic is an ideal solution to the problem.

Book-Ends

Sheet-plastic book-ends like the ones in Illus. 66 are simple to make. Cut two pieces of sheet about 10″ × 6″ (250 × 150 mm.) each. Heat and fold a right angle 3″ (75 mm.) from the end of each. This section goes under the books.

There are many things you can do with the upright sections. Cut off a corner as in Illus. 66; or make a design by drilling a series of holes; or cut a hole or geometrical design into them.

Painting also allows you a variety of options. The book-ends in Illus. 66 were painted with black acrylic paint. A piece of masking tape put in place before painting produced the neat clean line between the painted and unpainted parts. Always leave on masking tape until the paint is thoroughly dry.

Recipe Card Holder

This card holder is a handy item for a cook. It elevates a recipe card for reading, and protects it from splashing food (Illus. 67).

To make a holder to fit 5″ × 8″ (125 × 200 mm.) recipe cards, cut out a 15″ × 8″ (375 × 200 mm.) piece of $\frac{1}{8}$″ (3 mm.) thick sheet. Smooth and finish any rough edges, and remove the masking paper. Strip-heat and fold the strip back on itself along a line 5″ (125 mm.) from one end. Then, strip-heat and fold a right angle along a line 5″ (125 mm.) from the other end. Let it cool and your recipe holder is ready to use.

To make one to fit 3″ × 5″ (75 × 125 mm.) recipe cards, cut the sheet to measure 9″ × 5″ (225 × 125 mm.) and fold 3″ (75 mm.) from either end.

Cookbook Holder

A cookbook holder such as the one in Illus. 68 will be a big help in the kitchen as it holds a book open to a particular recipe while you are working.

Begin your project by cutting a piece of sheet plastic 24″ × 10″ (600 × 250 mm.). Mark lines dividing the strip into sections with widths of 4″ (100 mm.), 3″ (75 mm.), 9″ (225 mm.), and 8″ (200 mm.). After finishing and smoothing the edges, strip-heat and bend the three opposing right angles as shown in the illustration.

If you want to make a book holder for books which are thinner than most cookbooks, decrease the 3″ (75 mm.) measurement accordingly. This holder can be used for any book that has directions that you have to follow carefully—even this book!

Towel Rack

The dimensions to use for this project are determined by where you plan to hang it and what kind of towels it will hold. The rack in Illus. 69 was made from a strip of sheet plastic measuring 36″ × 1½″ (900 × 37.5 mm.).

After cutting the strip, smooth and finish any rough edges. Then, drill a hole 1″ (25 mm.) from each end of the strip, midway between the two edges of the strip. After removing the masking paper, draw two lines across at both ends with either a soft-tip ink marker or a china-marking pencil. Draw one 3″ (75 mm.) and another 6″ (150 mm.) from the ends. Finally, strip-heat and bend a right angle along each of these lines as shown in the photo.

Illus. 68. You will never add basil to an apple pie again with this handy cookbook holder, which will keep the pages from flipping while your head is turned.

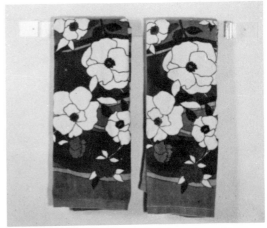

Illus. 69. A sheet-plastic towel rack will put an end to the rusty, discolored, hard-to-clean one you may have now.

Illus. 70. Bric-a-brac shelf.

Illus. 71. Mirror shelf.

Illus. 72. Heavy-duty shelf.

Shelves

There are any number of different shelves which can be made easily with sheet plastic. While all of the shelves pictured were made with transparent sheet, any of the various colored sheets available would be very attractive. The dimensions mentioned are only suggestions, for you will want to let the use and placement of your shelf determine its size.

Bric-a-brac Shelf

To make the shelf shown in Illus. 70, cut a piece of sheet plastic measuring 13″ × 9″ (335 × 225 mm.). You can round off one the of ends of the sheet as in Illus. 70, or leave it square.

To lay out a rounded end, use a compass, or trace a round object of the correct size on the masking paper before removing it from the sheet. Then cut out the half-circle. After drilling a hang-hole in the middle near the top, smooth and finish any rough edges.

Last, remove the masking paper, strip-heat, and bend a right angle along a line 3″ (75 mm.) from the *square* end.

Mirror Shelf

For this project, cut a piece of sheet that is about 3″ (75 mm.) wider and 7″ (175 mm.) longer than the mirror you plan to mount. This will allow for an equal border all round the mirror of 1½″ (37.5 mm.). Round off all four corners, either by cutting, filing, or sanding. Then, smooth and finish any rough edges.

Next, decide which method you are going to use to hang your shelf, and see page 19 to complete it.

After fixing your project so that it can be hung, peel off the masking paper. Then, strip-heat and bend a right angle along a line 4″ (100 mm.) from one of the ends. Finally, glue on the mirror, using any household cement, leaving the same margin on all sides.

Heavy-Duty Shelf

For this project, begin by cutting a piece of sheet plastic 22″ × 14″ (550 × 350 mm.). Then, drill a hole at each of the four corners, positioning it 1″ (25 mm.) in from the edges (Illus. 72).

After finishing and smoothing any rough edges, peel off all the masking paper. Then, measuring from one end, put marks at 3″, 10″, 12″, and 19″ (75, 250, 300, and 475 mm.) and, with a soft-tip ink marker or china-marking pencil, draw parallel lines across the sheet at these points. This will give you sections that are 3″, 7″, 2″, 7″, and 3″ (75, 175, 50, 175, and 75 mm.) long. Next, strip-heat and fold right angles facing one another along the middle two lines—those you marked off at 10″ (250 mm.) and at 12″ (300 mm.). Repeat the same process on each of the outside two lines—those you marked off at 3″ (75 mm.) and 19″ (475 mm.) —only now fold in the *opposite* direction. When the folds cool, your shelf is ready to hang.

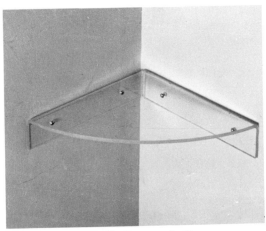

Illus. 73. Corner shelf.

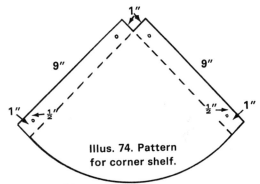

Illus. 74. Pattern for corner shelf.

Corner Shelf

To make a corner shelf, begin by first cutting a piece of sheet plastic into a square, the dimensions of which are determined by the depth you want to give the shelf. The shelf in Illus. 73, which is a convenient size, was made from a 10″ × 10″ (250 × 250 mm.) square. On two adjacent sides, draw lines 1″ (25 mm.) in and parallel to each edge, like the dotted lines in Illus. 74. These two lines will intersect, forming a 1″ (25 mm.) square at one corner of the sheet.

Next, lay out the curved edge of your shelf. Place the point of a compass where the two lines you drew intersect, and mark out a curve from edge to edge, forming a quarter of a circle. If you don't have a compass with enough span, tie a piece of string round your marker and hold the other end with your finger at the point where the two lines intersect.

Now, cut out the curve and the 1″ (25 mm.) square formed by the intersecting lines. Also drill the four holes shown in Illus. 74, that are 1″ (25 mm.) in and ½″ (12.5 mm.) over from each edge. Smooth off and finish any rough edges. Remove the masking paper. Strip-heat and bend right angles along the two lines. As soon as it cools, your shelf will be ready to attach to the corner of your walls.

You can also make a triangular corner shelf by using a straightedge front instead of a curved one. Simply draw a straight line where you would otherwise make a curved one and cut along it.

Utility Shelf

To make a utility shelf such as the one shown in Illus. 75 for holding anything from dinnerware to tools, begin by cutting a 12″ × 17½″ (300 × 437.5 mm.) piece of sheet plastic. Also, cut four 3″ (75 mm.) sections of ¼″ (6 mm.) thick rod. Draw a line parallel to the 17½″ (437.5 mm.) side, that is 4″ (100 mm.) in from it. At 3½″ (87.5 mm.) intervals along this line, drill holes that are the same diameter as your rods.

Then, after smoothing and finishing any rough edges, peel off the masking paper. Now, strip-heat and bend a right angle along a line parallel to the 17½″ (437.5 mm.) side. It should be 6″ (150 mm.) from the bottom side which will make it

Illus. 76. Bracket shelf.

2″ (50 mm.) above the row of holes. Next, to form a lip for the front of the shelf, bend another right angle along a line 1″ (25 mm.) in from the edge.

Make a right angle bend right at the midway point of each of the 3″ (75 mm.) rods. When cool, insert one end of each hook into a hole and glue it with solvent cement.

Finally, decide where you want to mount your shelf, and drill holes through it so that you can attach it to the wall with screws.

Bracket Shelf

To build a bracket shelf of the size shown in Illus. 76, begin by cutting two pieces of sheet plastic 10½″ × 6″ (262.5 × 150 mm.), and a third piece 24″ × 7½″ (600 × 187.5 mm.). From one corner on each of the 10½″ × 6″ (262.5 × 150 mm.) pieces, measure 3″ (75 mm.) along the edges in each direction and make a mark. Draw a diagonal

Illus. 75. Utility shelf.

line connecting these two points. Cut along this line, removing and discarding the small triangular section.

Next, at the other end of both of these sheets, drill a hole near each corner, 1″ (25 mm.) in from each edge. Remove the masking paper on both pieces, strip-heat and bend a right angle along a line 3″ (75 mm.) from the end on each.

Once they have cooled, your brackets can be attached to a wall, and the 24″ × 7½″ (600 × 187.5 mm.) piece laid on top. You can also glue it fast, if you wish, using solvent cement.

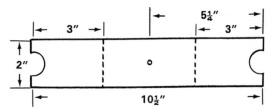

Illus. 78. Pattern for candlestick holder. Strip-heat and bend along dotted lines.

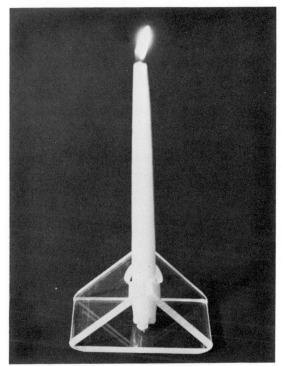

Illus. 77. Candlestick holder.

Candlestick Holder

To make the candlestick holder in Illus. 77, cut a piece of sheet plastic measuring 10½″ × 2″ (262.5 × 50 mm.). In the middle of the edges at either end on this strip, cut out a semi-circle the width of the candles you plan to use. Also drill a small hole right at the mid-point of the strip. This hole will be directly below the candle in the finished holder.

After finishing any rough edges and removing the masking paper, strip-heat along a line 3″ (75 mm.) from one end, and bend a 45° angle. Now do the same along a line 3″ (75 mm.) from the other end. You may have to re-heat and re-bend one or both angles so that the edges with the semi-circular cuts come together correctly.

Last, insert a pin or thin nail through the small hole and glue it in place. Force the candle down onto this pin. If the head of the pin or nail makes the bottom of the holder uneven, you may have to remove the pin and, using a larger drill bit, countersink the hole.

You may be so pleased with your candle holder that you will want to make another one so you can have a pair of them.

Illus. 79. An elegant pencil tray is easy to make and will hold, not only your pencils, but all kinds of small desk needs.

Pencil Tray

Constructing a small tray like the one shown in Illus. 79 is a simple project. Start with a 10″ × 6″ (250 × 150 mm.) piece of sheet plastic. Next, along all four sides of the sheet, draw a line 1½″ (37.5 mm.) from each edge, parallel to it. Two lines will intersect at each corner, forming a 1½″ (37.5 mm.) square. Cut out and discard the square at each of the four corners.

Smooth and finish any rough edges, remove the masking paper, and with a soft-tip ink marker or china-marking pencil, again lay out the same four lines, parallel to the edges, 1½″ (37.5 mm.) from them. Now, strip-heat and bend a right angle along each of these lines. Make sure that the line is exactly centered over the middle of the strip heater, so that each will bend in the same way with all of the corners meeting properly.

Serving Tray

Except for cutting out the hand-holes, the serving tray in Illus. 81 was fashioned in exactly the same way as the pencil tray (Illus. 79). To make a serving tray, begin with a piece of sheet plastic about 24″ × 15″ (600 × 375 mm.). Again, lay out four lines parallel to the four edges, each one 2″ (50 mm.) from the edge. Cut away and discard the four squares at the corners.

Lay out the hand-holes on separate paper or cardboard and cut them out to serve as a pattern. The holes should be 3″ × 1¼″ (75 × 31.25 mm.) with each end rounded into a semi-circle. Transfer

Illus. 81. You can make this serving tray almost as easily as the pencil tray in Illus. 79.

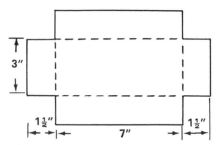

| 3″ |
| 1½″ | 7″ | 1½″ |

Illus. 80. Pattern for pencil tray. Strip-heat and bend along dotted lines.

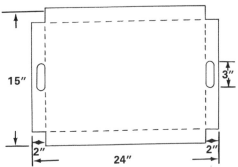

Illus. 82. Pattern for serving tray. Strip-heat and bend along dotted lines.

the pattern to the masking paper with the inside (bottom) edge of the hole running along the line you drew previously to cut the squares.

Drill one or two large holes in the middle of each hand-hole drawing, then use a coping saw to cut along the outline. Carefully smooth and finish any rough edges or uneven cuts. Round the edges of the holes slightly to make carrying more comfortable. For the rest of the project, follow the instructions for the pencil tray (see page 40), starting with the removal of the masking paper.

By varying the measurements to conform to the size of a loaf of bread, you can make an attractive bread or roll "basket," following the same procedures.

Pencil Holder

To make a pencil holder like the one shown in Illus. 83, cut a strip of sheet plastic 11″ × 2″ (275 × 50 mm.), and two pieces of sheet 3″ (75 mm.) square. Round holes with a 2″ (50 mm.) diameter were cut into these square side pieces for the holder pictured in Illus. 83, but you can cut out any shapes, such as squares or triangles; or paint designs on the square side pieces.

Remove the masking paper on the long strip. Mark lines across the strip 4″ (100 mm.) from each end and strip-heat along each line. Then, bend a right angle along each line. Before these bends cool, check to see that your side pieces fit properly. If they do not, make the necessary adjustments.

Finally, after removing the masking paper from one surface of each of the side pieces, clamp the unmasked side of each to either side of the bent strip as shown in Illus. 83, and glue them together using solvent glue and the capillary method (see page 17).

Illus. 83. This pencil holder is made of one strip of sheet plastic that has been heated and bent twice to form the base and ends, and two square pieces that form the sides.

Illus. 84. This vase is much easier to make than it looks. Just follow the bending directions in Illus. 85.

Vase

Make this simple holder for dried flowers by heatforming four bends on a piece of sheet plastic 24″ × 8″ (60 × 200 mm.). Each bend should form a 60° angle. Illus. 85 shows the progression of the heating and bending, as well as the appropriate measurements for the bends.

Double Candle Holder

To make a holder that will hold two candles, such as the one shown in Illus. 86, begin by cutting a strip of sheet plastic 18″ × 2″ (450 × 50 mm.). Drill or cut a hole of slightly larger diameter than the candles you plan to use 7″ (175 mm.) from each

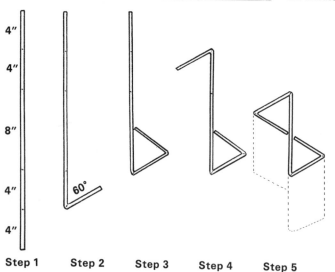

4″

4″

8″

4″

60°

4″

Step 1   Step 2   Step 3   Step 4   Step 5

Illus. 85. Remember when you are following these steps that you are looking at the edge of the sheet. Step 5 shows a scheme of the finished vase.

42

Illus. 86. This double candle holder requires four bends.

Knife Rack

The knife rack in Illus. 87 was designed for medium-size carving knives. If you want to build a rack for larger knives, or smaller ones, alter the measurements accordingly, but keep the same proportions.

To begin, cut a $15'' \times 7\frac{1}{2}''$ (375 × 187.5 mm.) piece of sheet plastic. Smooth and finish any rough edges. Next, drill small holes for hanging the rack $1''$ (25 mm.) in from the edges at each of the corners along one of the $7\frac{1}{2}''$ (187.5 mm.) edges.

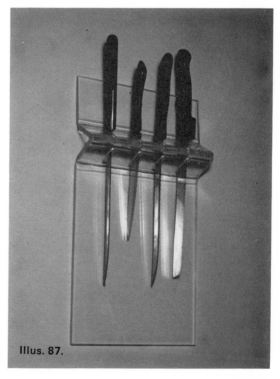

Illus. 87.

end of the strip and midway between the two edges.

After you have smoothed any rough edges and removed the masking, lay out, strip-heat and bend four right angles: one $3''$ (75 mm.) and one $5''$ (125 mm.) from each end of the strip.

Finally, mark a point near the end of the folded bottom strip directly beneath the middle of each of the holes you cut. At this spot, drill a small hole and glue in a pin or thin nail which will serve to hold the bottom of each candle in place.

Illus. 88. Measuring where to strip-heat for the first bend.

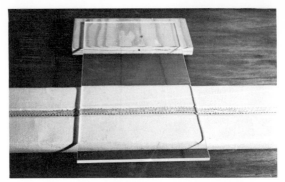

Illus. 89. Strip heating the first bend.

Once all the masking paper has been removed, lay out a line across the width of the sheet, 4″ (100 mm.) in from the end where you drilled the holes (see Illus. 88). Strip-heat along this line (Illus. 89), and then fold the sheet completely back upon itself. You will need to firmly clamp the folded sheet in this position until it cools (Illus. 90). Use wooden strips or cardboard to protect the plastic from the clamps as shown.

Now, lay out the four slots for your knives. Make each slot considerably wider than the knife blade it will hold. For large carving knives, cut each slot at least $1\frac{1}{2}$″ (37.5 mm.) long. The four slots should be $1\frac{1}{2}$″ (37.5 mm.) apart, with the same distance between the end slot and the edge. Each slot should end at least $\frac{1}{2}$″ (12.5 mm.) in from the fold you made, as in Illus. 91. To protect the plastic while you cut the slots, cover about 2″

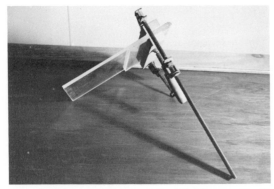

Illus. 90. After folding the sheet back upon itself, clamp it firmly until it cools.

Illus. 91. Measuring where to cut the slots for the knives.

Illus. 92. You can use masking tape to protect the area round the slots during cutting.

Illus. 93. Drilling holes to start the slots.

(50 mm.) of the sheet closest to the folded edge with masking tape.

Drill a $\frac{1}{4}''$ (6 mm.) or $\frac{3}{8}''$ (10 mm.) hole at each end of the line where a slot is to go. Then, using a coping or a hack-saw, cut through between the two holes (Illus. 94). After cutting, use a small file to smooth the edges of each slot. (During the drilling and cutting, small chips of plastic will probably be trapped in the fold, but you can remove them after the next step.)

Next, strip-heat *the same fold*, but this time place the fold above and parallel to the strip heater as in Illus. 95. As it softens, the folded sections will

Illus. 94. Cutting the slots with a hack-saw. The blade has been entered sideways.

Illus. 95. Repeat the strip heating to open the fold.

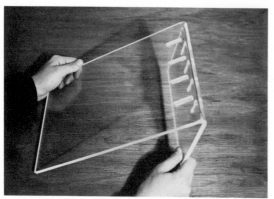
Illus. 96. Allow the fold to open this far. Then cool it.

Illus. 97. After another heating, a second fold is completed.

begin to separate. When they have separated as much as shown in Illus. 96 (about 50°), either clamp the sheet in this position, or cool it in water.

Now, strip-heat two lines, each 2″ (50 mm.) in opposite directions from, but parallel to, the fold you just made. Along *each* line, make a 110° bend, or make the two bends so that both of the unslotted sections of the sheet lie in the same flat plane as shown in Illus. 99.

Your knife rack is now ready to hang. If you have knives all the same length, you may want to fold a straight narrow shelf on the bottom of the rack for the tips of the knives to rest on.

Illus. 98. Strip heating for the third and last time.

Illus. 99. Your knife rack is complete.

Suppliers

(Note: In England, Australia, and New Zealand, sheet plastic is known as "Oroglas.")

Index